RAIN FOREST

MICHAEL GEORGE

CREATIVE EDITIONS

Designed by Rita Marshall
with the help of Thomas Lawton

Published in 1993 by Creative Editions
123 South Broad Street
Mankato, Minnesota 56001

Creative Editions is an imprint of
Creative Education, Inc. This title is
published as a joint effort between
Creative Education, Inc. and American
Education Publishing.

Photography by Peter Arnold,
Gary Braasch, Wolfgang Kaehler,
Minden Pictures, and Tom Stack

Library of Congress
Cataloging-in-Publication Data

George, Michael, 1964–
Rain forests / by Michael George.
Summary: Discusses where tropical rain
forests are found and what kind of life
they support.
ISBN 1-56846-062-7
1. Rain forest ecology—Juvenile
literature. 2. Rain forests—Juvenile
literature. [1. Rain
forests. 2. Rain forest ecology.
3. Ecology] I. Title.   91-16875
QH541.5.R27G46   1991
574.5'2642—dc20

In Memory of
GEORGE R. PETERSON, SR.

7

Most people imagine tropical rain forests as the settings for adventure movies, filled with peculiar plants, vicious animals, and savage ape-men. Yet despite their attempts, moviemakers cannot portray the excitement of an actual tropical *Rain Forest*. It is more amazing than anything that can be shown on a screen.

Rain forest in Costa Rica.

8

Upon entering a tropical rain forest, you smell the aroma of flowers and hear the singing of birds. At first, the forest appears damp, dark, and gloomy. But as your eyes adjust to the dim forest interior, you notice brightly colored flowers amid striking shades of green. Everywhere you look there are creatures creeping, crawling, jumping, and flying. Monkeys swing through the trees, ants parade across the ground, and butterflies flutter through the air. The tropical rain forest is filled with an extravaganza of wonderful, beautiful life.

A waterfall in a Tahiti forest.
Inset: A pangolin.

Tropical rain forests are appropriately named—they are all located in tropical regions of the Earth, between the Tropic of Cancer and the Tropic of Capricorn. They cover large areas of Central and South America, Asia, Africa, and many islands in the Pacific Ocean. The *Amazon* is the largest tropical rain forest in the world. It covers a region in South America that is nearly as large as the continental United States.

The Amazon rain forest.

Located near the equator, tropical rain forests do not have seasons as most people know them. The temperature stays near 80 degrees Fahrenheit, summer and winter, and plants are green all year long. Rather than being defined by average temperatures, seasons in the tropics are determined by the amount of rainfall. Over an entire year, most tropical forests receive more than eighty inches of precipitation. Most of this moisture falls during the rainy season, when water may pour from the sky for days on end. Although there is less precipitation during the dry season, there are still drenching rains every few days.

Rain in the jungle.
Inset: Passion flower.

Blessed with warm temperatures and abundant rainfall, the tropical forest has a climate that is ideal for life. As a result, an astonishing variety of organisms inhabit tropical forests. In fact, of all the known species of plants and animals in the world, about half live in tropical rain forests. From beneath the forest floor to the tops of the tallest trees, tropical forests teem with life.

A quetzal leaves the nest.

15

In order to classify and study this abundance of life, scientists divide tropical forests into four main levels: ground, low forest, mid-forest, and canopy. Each level of the forest has its own characteristic vegetation and animal life.

Unusual vegetation.

Ground Level is the lowest layer of the tropical rain forest. Many people assume that the only way to travel through a rain forest is by swinging a machete, hacking through thick vines and vegetation. This image, however, is not typical of tropical rain forests. In most areas, a thick covering of leaves, suspended high in the air, prevents sunlight from reaching the ground. Since plants cannot grow without sunlight, most of the forest floor has little vegetation. The ground is covered by only a thin layer of dead leaves.

Although the forest floor is generally bare, thick undergrowth does occur along the edges of the forest, on river banks, and in isolated clearings. In these areas sunlight slices through the thick covering of forest leaves, and an uprush of plants struggles for survival.

The forest floor.

19

Whether it is bare or entangled with vegetation, the forest floor is inhabited by many interesting and important creatures. Most of the organisms that live on the ground are *Decomposers,* tiny creatures that feed on dead plant and animal materials. They include a variety of insects, bacteria, and fungi. These organisms are so abundant that dead leaves and small animals rarely remain on the ground for more than a day.

Ants work to clean the floor.
Inset: A metallic beetle.

In addition to these tiny housekeepers, the forest floor is also inhabited by a variety of larger creatures. Elephants, hippopotamuses, and water buffaloes live on the floor of the African and Asian rain forests. The ground level of the Amazon forest houses smaller animals, including armadillos, coatimundis, and a variety of tropical rodents. The most ferocious inhabitant of the Amazon forest floor is the *Peccary,* a wild pig armed with razor-sharp tusks. After nightfall, packs of peccaries roam the forest in search of food.

An armadillo.

23

Located a few feet above the ground is the *Low-level Forest*. Here, colonies of insects live among odd-looking bushes and shrubs that are found no place else on Earth. Most plants in the low-level forest have broad, leathery leaves. The wide leaves help the plants absorb what little light there is in the dim forest interior. Unlike the bushes of temperate forests, tropical shrubs are unusually large; many species grow to the size of mature apple trees. Even tropical grasses are oversized— *Bamboo*, a type of grass that thrives in East African forests, can grow as tall as a four-story building.

Page 22: A broad leaf.
Page 23: Bamboo in Hawaii.

Above the plants of the low-level forest, slender tree trunks stretch toward the sky. Covered with mosses and lichens, the tree trunks provide ideal hiding places for tropical insects. Many of these creatures are so well camouflaged that they are nearly invisible. However, the *Mid-level Forest* is also patrolled by keen-eyed birds looking for a tasty snack. Many of these tropical birds are decorated with blue, yellow, green, and red feathers. The brilliant colors help the birds blend in with the forest's flowers and leaves. The colors also help the birds attract mates.

Mid-level growth.
Inset: A parrot.

Located above the open spaces of the mid-level forest is the *Canopy*, the topmost level of a tropical forest. The canopy itself contains various layers of vegetation. The lowest layer hangs fifty or sixty feet above the ground. These leaves are usually so thick that a person on the forest floor cannot see through them. The middle layer of the canopy consists of taller trees, species that stretch up to one hundred feet above the ground. Beyond this thin layer of leaves lies the upper canopy, the highest level of a tropical forest. Here, trees up to two hundred feet tall tower above the dense lower canopies.

View toward the canopy.

28

Bathed in warm sunshine, the forest canopy differs greatly from the dark and gloomy forest interior. Besides receiving more sunlight, the top of the forest also receives more moisture than the forest floor. Some of the rain that falls on a tropical forest never reaches the ground, because it is absorbed by the leaves and branches of the canopy trees.

The canopy also differs from the forest interior in that it is caressed by warm tropical breezes. In order to withstand the stronger winds that accompany storms, canopy trees have developed unusual methods of support. The tallest trees have wide, winglike extensions at the bases of their trunks. These extensions, called *Buttresses*, help support the tall trunks and heavy branches. Other trees have pitchfork-like roots that provide extra stability in wet, swampy soils.

Page 28: Canopy in bloom.
Page 29: Buttressed tree.

Tropical trees are also reinforced by *Lianas,* cablelike vines that are tangled in the leaves and branches of the canopy. Some of these vines are as thick as telephone poles, and many are hundreds of feet long. Lianas are so strong that when the tree breaks off at its base, it often remains standing, suspended by the vines.

Trees and lianas are not the only plants that make up the forest canopy. Many smaller plants actually grow on the branches and leaves of the canopy trees. Scientists call these plants *Epiphytes,* or *Air Plants.* They include a wide variety of orchids, ferns, and bromeliads—tropical plants that are related to the pineapple.

Vines in the rain forest of Africa.

Suspended high above the ground, epiphytes take advantage of the canopy's abundant sunshine and moisture. Rather than burrowing into the ground, an epiphyte's roots wrap around tree trunks and branches. The roots anchor the plant to the canopy and absorb moisture from the humid forest air. They also extract nutrients from the debris that collects in the crooks and crannies of tree limbs. Besides nourishing epiphytes, this treetop soil shelters a variety of animals, including spiders, insects, and even earthworms.

Epiphytes in the canopy.
Inset: A tropical butterfly in Brazil.

Insects and other small animals are not the only creatures that inhabit the forest canopy. In fact, of all the creatures that live in the Amazon rain forest, more than half reside in the canopy. The treetops house an assortment of monkeys, birds, frogs, snakes, and lizards. Some of these animals never venture to the ground below. Night and day, the canopy is filled with the sounds of animals.

From the forest floor to the canopy treetops, the tropical rain forest is filled with a fascinating variety of organisms. All of these creatures depend on each other in intricate ways. Trees need lianas for support, many animals require plants for food, and all the organisms depend on decomposers to return important nutrients to the soil. But with so many organisms living in one place, there is also fierce competition for food and space. Survival in a tropical forest is a difficult game. Another enemy is lurking behind every leaf.

A tree python waits.

For survival in the forest, speed and strength are helpful, but they are not always enough. Staying alive also requires keen senses and effective methods of finding food and avoiding enemies. Some creatures fool their enemies with unusual disguises. Other forest animals are *Camouflaged*. By blending into the surroundings, they increase both their chances of finding food and their chances of avoiding enemies. Rather than trying to hide, many poisonous animals do all they can to be noticed. They display brilliant colors to warn enemies of their unpleasant taste.

Within the tropical rain forest some species are friends, and some are enemies, but all the creatures depend on each other in many ways. Because of this intricate balance, tropical rain forests have endured for hundreds of millions of years, longer than any other habitat on Earth. Unfortunately, the future of the Earth's tropical rain forests is not guaranteed.

Page 36: A poison dart frog.
Page 37: A lemur.

In a quest for lumber and farmland, human-kind is destroying the Earth's tropical rain forests. Every minute, bulldozers and fires clear another fifty acres of tropical land. The nutrients that are necessary for life are burned or are carried away in trucks. Any nutrients that remain are washed away by the daily rains. Lacking these important nu-trients, the land cannot be reforested, and the soil cannot support crops for more than two or three seasons. Once destroyed, a tropical forest is lost forever, along with countless species of plants and animals. All that re-mains is barren, lifeless soil.

Page 38: Slash-and-burn agriculture.
Page 39: A man prepares to plant corn.

DATE DUE

T110			
MAY 2 4 1995			
SEP 1 4 1995			
SEP 2 2 10b			
SEP 2 8 103			
DEC 0 5 114			
MAY 20 '96 5			
DE 1 X '96			
AP 7 '98 103			
AP 1 4 '98 103			
T-103			
SE 28 '00			